The Most Loved Books

By Jackie Dennis

Illustrated by Meredith Hancock

CREDITS

The Most Loved Books

Written by Jackie Dennis
Illustrated by Meredith Hancock

PUBLISHED BY

© December 2020 Jackie Dennis
ISBN: 978-1-953440-02-0
Library of Congress Control Number: 2014353890

Dedication

To all the authors who have inspired me over the years while reading your books to my children, and of course, to my children and grandchildren, who continue to inspire me every day.

Robbi and Jacob were helping Grammy move.

"Come on guys, let's head up to the attic," said Grammy.

"I'll be up after I put these boxes in the moving van," Daddy said.

The attic looked the same
as Robbi remembered.
The trunk was still in the corner.
"I can't believe you've been to all these places,"
said Robbi, as she looked at all the stickers
covering the trunk. She opened it.

"Oh, I used to love to wear this.
I would pretend I was going to the ball that you went to in Paris with the Count of Avalon."
Robbi put the hat on. She held up a beautiful dress and swirled with it in front of her.

Jacob headed over to the bookshelf shaped like a red caboose. The books on the top shelf had beautiful covers that looked almost new. The middle shelf had a pile of old magazines, and on the very bottom shelf, in the very bottom corner, was a stack of three old, tattered books.

Some were missing their covers and had dingy yellow pages. Others were missing pages and had spots of who-knows-what on the covers.

Jacob picked them up. They had a funny smell, but Jacob kind of liked it. Sinking down cross- legged on the floor, he started to flip through the pages.

When he had been quiet for a long time, Robbi finally noticed what he was doing.
"Jacob put those down," she said.
"They are disgusting looking.
They're all covered with dust and they stink!"

"You're not the boss of me!" Jacob said. Grammy took the books from Jacob and hugged them close to her chest. "I'd forgotten these were here. They were your Daddy's favorites."

Robbi looked at the books more closely. "Daddy didn't take very good care of them," she said. "Didn't he like them?"

"Oh, quite the opposite," said Grammy. "They were loved too much. Every night at bedtime, these were the books your Daddy asked for. He had so many books to choose from, but night after night, he picked the same three books."

"We would read them in the winter
drinking cocoa by the fire,
in the summer drinking lemonade by the pool,
up north after making angels in the snow,
and down south
after making castles on the beach.

These books have been everywhere.
That's why they are so tattered and torn.
Not because no one loved them,
but because they were the most loved books
in the world! When your Daddy opened these
books, he was whisked away to magical places
where bunnies talked, and monkeys flew."

Just then Daddy came up the attic stairs. "Is there anything up here we are taking with us?"

"I'd like to take this trunk of old dresses," said Robbi.

"Okay," said Daddy.

"How about you, Jacob?"
"Can I have these books?" Jacob asked.
Daddy looked at the books, smiled and rumpled Jacob's hair. "That would be great."

Later that night, after Grammy was settled into her new bedroom, Robbi and Jacob came in to say goodnight.

Jacob pulled the three books from behind his back.

"Grammy", Robbi asked, "Could you read these books to us?"

Grammy patted the bed beside her.
In the softest voice ever, Grammy spoke.

"Come up here. Let me take you to your Daddy's favorite places."

Grammy slowly opened the book, and once again, like so many years before, the magic began.

About the Author

Jackie is the mom of five children and currently has seven grandchildren. She lives in Nokesville, Virginia with her husband, George, two sons, six rescue pets (and counting), and bookshelves full of her children's MOST LOVED BOOKS.

Photo by Sherry Dornblaser

More books from RSP Press

Available at rsplaunchpad.com

CPSIA information can be obtained
at www.ICGtesting.com
Printed in the USA
LVHW020910221121
703847LV00004B/34